STRANGE
BUT TRUE
DOGS

SWEETWATER
    PRESS

Strange But True Dogs

Copyright © 2006 by Sweetwater Press
Produced by Cliff Road Books

ISBN-13: 978-1-58173-620-5
ISBN-10: 1-58173-620-7

Cover design by McGinty
Book design by Pat Covert

Printed in Italy

STRANGE BUT TRUE DOGS

SWEETWATER
PRESS

CONTENTS

RECORD SETTERS: DOGS THAT CAN'T BE BEAT

A greyhound named Bang once jumped 30 feet while chasing a hare at Brecon Lodge in England. He cleared a 4-foot, 6-inch gate and landed on the pavement, breaking a bone.

In 2000, a group of 210 huskies pulled a 145,002-pound flatbed trailer and mine drill for 6 blocks.

Although he died in 1945, a Yorkshire terrier from England still holds the world record for being the smallest dog. He was only 2.5 inches tall, 3.5 inches long, and weighed 4 ounces.

Another record-breaking tiny dog, Ondra, died in 2002. The terrier was accidentally given a shot of the wrong medicine at a vet clinic in the Czech Republic. Ondra was 4.7 inches tall.

This superhero thing is getting old.

The largest dog team to ever pull a load was 230 dogs in 1999.

The largest litter of dogs ever born was 23 puppies—a feat which 3 different dogs have accomplished.

Baked at the People's Company Bakery in Minneapolis, the world's largest dog biscuit was 7.7 feet long, 1.9 feet wide, and 1 inch thick.

Gibson, a Great Dane, holds the record for being the world's tallest dog. In 2004, he was measured at 42.2 inches.

An English Mastiff named Hercules had a 38-inch neck.

The world's heaviest dog was an English Mastiff named Zorba, who was 343 pounds at just 8 years old.

In 2003, a group of people outside of Edinburgh attempted to break the world record for dog-walking.

Thousands of pets and their owners showed up, hoping to raise money for the University of Edinburgh Dick Vet Small Animal Hospital, but fell shy of the world record—which was 3,118 dogs.

My personal growth counselor says this will bring inner peace.

I wish I'd bought a hybrid.

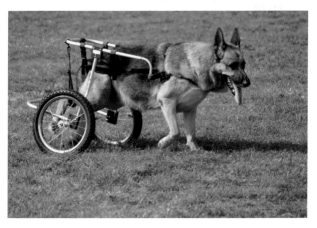

In a 2002 Harvard University study, dogs outperformed chimps on certain cognitive tests.

U.S. Customs Labrador "Snag" has busted criminals out of $810 million worth of drugs.

The Poodle is one of the smartest breeds in the world.

One tiny canine, Chanda-Leah, knows more than 1,000 tricks.

An Australian cattle dog named Bluey lived longer than any other dog in the world—a whopping 29 years.

The world's longest fence is called The Dog Fence, which prevents wild dingoes from killing sheep in Australia. At 6,000 miles, it is 1,000 miles longer than the Great Wall of China.

Watch out! German Shepherds bite more people than any other breed.

Mr. Jeffries, a British Basset hound, holds the record for the longest ears ever—an incredible 29.2 centimeters.

I hope my wife understands this is all part of being an actor.

A dog named Sig was once reported by CNN to act like a kangaroo and jump up to 6 feet in the air while on walks with his owner.

The Shar-Pei (pronounced Shah-Pay) appeared in the *Guinness Book of World Records* as the most rare dog in the world for 3 consecutive years in the early 1970s. They are no longer that close to extinction.

Can't a dog get any work done
around here?

A 20-month old Kelpie was purchased
for $5,400 at a Victorian auction in
2006, and is believed to be the most
expensive working dog in the world.

Do you have any collateral?

In October 2004, *Scooby-Doo* was awarded a Guinness World Record for the most episodes of a cartoon comedy series. Its winning episode was number 350—"A Scooby-Doo Halloween."

The world's largest annual dog show is Crufts. In 1991, when being held at the National Exhibition Center in Birmingham, England, the show received 22,993 entries for participating pups.

A German Shepherd guide dog named Orient once led a blind hiker through the entire 2,100-mile Appalachian Trail.

The fastest dog in the country, Juice, a Border Collie, can slalom through 60 poles in 12.3 seconds.

In 2003, more than half of the dogs in the United States knew some sort of trick. That is more than 25.3 million dogs amazing their owners.

Ashrita Furman once hopped 206 times on a pogo stick while holding his dog.

So I'm a fairy—you wanna make something of it?

A dog named Abra once dug a hole 11 feet deep.

Anything for a quarter pounder.

MY HERO: BRAVE LITTLE PUPS

The world's only police dog with a perfect record for sniffing out drugs was General W-235. He assisted in 220 searches and, of course, 220 arrests.

Where's the nearest phone booth?

The greatest number of drug seizures in a single year by dogs was 969. Rocky and Barco were patrolling the Texas/Mexico border at the time, and Mexican drug lords were offering $30,000 to anyone who could get rid of them.

Well, Mrs. Presky, there's a little water problem in the basement.

Dogs can sense chemical changes in the air that indicate their owner is ill or dying.

Dogs have been thought to detect cancer on more than one occasion.

Nancy Best's dog, Mia, buried her nose in Nancy's right breast multiple times before she finally felt for herself, found a lump, and was diagnosed with Stage II breast cancer.

In 1989, an article in a respected British medical journal reported that a dog constantly sniffed a mole on the back of its owner's leg until he had it checked out and was diagnosed with melanoma.

Because man was afraid to go into space for the first time, the first astronaut was a dog! Laikia was sent into space by the Russian government in 1957.

When an unfamiliar visitor comes into the home, the English Mastiff will place itself between its master and the stranger.

When William A. Ellerbrock was a young riverboat captain in the 1800s, he burned to death fighting a waterfront fire. His dog, Boss, also burned trying to save him. The two were buried together, and the local firefighter community erected a statue over the grave in honor of the brave little pup.

You dirty rat! I was going
to eat that poop!

America's first war dog, Stubby, was a Bull Terrier who was smuggled onto a war ship during World War I. The most decorated dog in history, he warned sleeping sailors of mustard gas attacks and even caught a German spy by biting him in the pants.

Not sure what I'm looking for but I'm positive something's there!

Stubby met Presidents Woodrow Wilson, Calvin Coolidge, and Warren G. Harding. The YMCA gave him a lifetime membership to their facilities, which consisted of "three bones a day and a place to sleep."

Stubby eventually became the mascot of Georgetown University. His remains are at the Smithsonian Museum in Washington, D.C.

In 1925, a Doberman Pinscher named Sauer tracked a thief one hundred miles across South Africa by scent alone.

Some dogs can detect an oncoming epileptic seizure in a person up to one hour beforehand.

Barry the St. Bernard saved at least forty people trapped in mountain snow at Great St. Bernard Pass. Today a monument stands in his honor at the famed Cimetiere des Chiens in France.

Barry's stuffed body was once on display at a Swiss Museum in Berne.

I'm just practicing. I have to bite some awfully fat people later.

Only one animal's testimony of evidence will stand up in court—the bloodhound, which is often used to track missing children, victims of natural disasters, and escaped convicts.

Jerry Allen Bradford of Pensacola, Florida, was injured when one of the puppies he was trying to kill put its paw on the trigger of a gun, shooting Jerry in the wrist.

When the ancient Roman community of Pompeii was excavated, researchers found the bones of a dog lying across a child as if it were trying to protect her.

A dog in Kenya once found an abandoned two-week-old girl in the forest, wrapped her in a cloth, carried her across a busy road, and dragged her under a barbed wire fence before placing her down amidst a litter of puppies. The dog's owner rushed the baby to the hospital and named her Angel.

Oh Mr. Disney...do I get the part?

When a Richland, Washington, woman fell out of her wheelchair, her dog, Faith, hit the 911 speed-dial button with her nose and barked into the receiver until a dispatcher sent help. Faith also opened the door when police arrived.

Bark softly and carry a javelin.

A 12-pound Yorkshire terrier once defended an old woman from a large attacking Akita. The pup only needed nine stitches when the battle was over.

Border Terriers are known to kill animals smaller than themselves, such as rabbits and cats.

The Doberman's tail is sometimes docked at birth so criminals cannot grab hold of it while the dog is working with police.

Guide dogs are taught to:
- Walk in a straight line unless there is an obstacle,
- Not turn corners unless commanded to,
- Stop at curbs, and
- Judge the height of entryways so their owner does not hit his or her head.

When Slavic invaders took over the German castle Ordensritterburg in the thirteenth century, a Hovawart rescued an infant. The boy, Eike von Repkow, grew up to become a historical legal figure in the country and made a law that any Hovawart killed or stolen must be either replaced or paid for by the person at fault.

The Philadelphia Mint bought its first canine employee, Nero, for $3 to protect the building. The Mint had a rule that no employee other than the night watchman could feed the dog for fear potential criminals would earn his liking.

Thanks for calling 1-800-I-H8-CATS.

Bred along the Chesapeake Bay to hunt waterfowl, the Chesapeake Bay Retriever not only ran after game for its master but also sat in the wagon at the market to make sure nothing was stolen that was going to be sold.

Look, I know we come from different backgrounds. Our families will have to understand.

Because of their sharp sense of smell, Beagles are used by the U.S. Department of Agriculture to sniff luggage for food being brought into the country illegally. Called the "Beagle Brigade," the dogs wear green jackets when they work.

Legend holds that Dutchman William The Silent's life was once saved when his Pug thwarted an assassination attempt. Pompey scratched his master, then jumped on his face when he saw the strange men coming towards the tent.

HEY! Slow traffic keep right!

Any intruder's nightmare, the Bandog,
kin to the American Mastiff and the Pit
Bull, are said to be insensible to pain.
Not a dog you want to go up against!

LIGHTS, CAMERA, FETCH: FAMOUS DOGS

The first dog to ever star in a movie was Blair, a Collie featured in *Rescued by Rover* (1905). The film was the first to associate dogs with the name Rover.

No autographs please.

Although portrayed as a female dog in the sitcom, Lassie was actually played by several male Collies because their coats of fur looked better on camera.

That's D-O-double-Gizzay to you.

Hollywood's first canine superstar,
Rin Tin Tin signed his own film contracts
with his paw print.

After staring in 27 black-and-white films,
Rin Tin Tin died in 1932. He made $5
million during his 14-year career.

Rin Tin Tin's movies saved Warner
Brothers Pictures from declaring
bankruptcy.

Soccer, a Jack Russell Terrier who portrayed the pup "Wishbone" in commercials, hated swimming, and had two stunt doubles.

In 1928, *Time* magazine featured its first Basset Hound on the front cover. The feature story was about the upcoming Westminster Kennel Club Dog Show at Madison Square Garden.

During the holidays, a pup named Providence works for the Salvation Army in Kansas. He takes donations to the kettle and even rings the bell.

You should see the shoes and hat.

Dogs have acted in plays since ancient times. Two thousand years ago, a Poodle named Zoppico was famous for eating a piece of meat and then falling over as if dead on stage. When the crowd applauded, he would leap back to life.

A dog at Fort Benning, Georgia, won the hearts of soldiers by walking like he was crippled when he wanted food. The troops called him "Calculator," because he "puts down three and carries one." The dog died after being poisoned in 1923.

So I go, like ... and he goes, like ... and then I go ...

It is rumored that Paris Hilton once rented her Chihuahua, Tinkerbell, her own hotel room for $250 a night.

Other stars who own Chihuahuas: Britney Spears (Bit-Bit), Adrien Brody (Ceelo), John Gebhardt (Scab), and Eminem (Smoky).

Mickey Mouse's sidekick, Goofy, was originally called Dippy Dawg.

After he set up the first smallpox vaccination clinics in China, Dr. Heuston of Ireland was gifted a pair of Pekinese by Chinese minister Li Hung Chang. When taken back to Ireland, the two pups—named Chang and Lady Li—became the first of their breed in the country.

Alicia Silverstone got her dog, Samson, a cameo in the movie *Clueless*.

Paul McCartney wrote the song "Martha My Dear" about his sheepdog.

McCartney also honored his dog when he recorded "A Day in the Life." At the close of the song, he recorded a high-pitched sound from an ultrasonic whistle. The note cannot be heard with human ears.

Bring on da noise, bring on da funk.

I love the '80s.

Made famous by the phrase "Yo Quiero Taco Bell," the Chihuahua from the Taco Bell commercials is female—not male as portrayed. Her real name is Gidget.

Other famous Chihuahuas include motivational "speaker" Wheely Willy, a fictional paraplegic dog and star of several children's books, and Bruiser, co-star of the film *Legally Blonde*.

Comic-strip star Garfield referred to pal Odie as "half-beagle, half-brick."

Pablo Picasso's dog, Lump, was said to have inspired some of his paintings.

A Chinese Crested dog named Sam won the World's Ugliest Dog Contest in California three years in a row. After appearing on several morning talk shows and websites in 2005, he was put down on his 15th birthday.

The Great Dane is the state dog of Pennsylvania. Hanna-Barbera's Scooby Doo, *The Jetson's* Astro, and comic strip star Marmaduke were all Great Danes.

The Basset Hound used in the Hush Puppy shoe commercials is named Jason.

In the March 12, 1992, episode of *The Simpsons*, Homer tells Bart that Adolf Hitler's German Shepherd Blondi is in "Doggie Hell."

Whaddup, dawg?

Moose, the Jack Russell Terrier that played "Eddie" on the sitcom *Frasier*, had a stunt double. His son, Enzo, often stepped in for the more demanding tricks. Both dogs appeared in the movie *My Dog Skip*.

Moose also appeared on the covers of *Entertainment Weekly* and *TV Guide*, and put out his own calendar.

In 2000, Moose's "autobiography," *My Life as a Dog*, appeared on bookshelves across the country.

A Bluetick Coonhound named Smokey
is the mascot of the University
of Tennessee.

Winner of the Doggie Elton John
Look-Alike Contest

Hmm, I thought running away from home would be easier than this.

President Lyndon Johnson owned Beagles named Him, Her, and Edgar.

Ronald Reagan's dog Lucky was a Bouvier des Flandres.

The Carolina Dog, which is really a wild American Dingo, may have been Fred Gipson's inspiration for *Old Yeller*.

Oprah Winfrey has two pet Cocker Spaniels—Solomon and Sophie.

Other famous spaniels include Lucky Bundy from *Married...with Children* and Lady from *Lady and the Tramp*.

The film *Because of Winn-Dixie* starred Berger Picards, a French breed that nearly went extinct after the two world wars. Today they are so rare that the dogs had to be shipped to the U.S. from France to make the movie.

Although it was never expected to be a hit, *Benji* (1974) made $40 million in the U.S. alone. Writer Joe Camp was inspired to write the series after watching *Lady and the Tramp*.

Bill Clinton loved his dog, Buddy, so much that he once said, "If you want a friend in Washington, you have to get a dog." Unfortunately, Buddy was hit by a car in New York in 2002.

I said heave to starboard, you stupid cat!

Betty Boop's boyfriend was a dog named Bimbo.

In the "Peanuts" cartoons, Snoopy's Beagle sister is named Belle.

She's super chic, super chic. She's super chic-y, yow.

English painter William Hogarth loved Pugs so much that he included them in several of his paintings of his wife and friends.

In the original *101 Dalmatians*, Pongo had 72 spots, Perdita had 68 spots, and each puppy had 32.

Toto from *The Wizard of Oz* was played by a female Cairn Terrier named Terry.

A man in a brown dog suit occasionally joined *Mr. Rogers' Neighborhood*. Kids across the country knew him as "Bob Dog."

Winston Churchill's wife called him by the nickname Pug. He even wrote a silly poem about his alter-ego:
Poor Puggy-wug
Oh, what is the matter with
poor Puggy-wug
Pet him and kiss him and give him a hug.
Run and fetch him a suitable drug,
Wrap him up tenderly all in a rug,
That is the way to cure Puggy-wug.

TOO HOT TO TROT: DOG HEALTH

One year in a dog's life is NOT equivalent to 7 human years. At 1 year, a dog is as healthy as a 16-year-old human; at 2 it is about 24; at 3 years it is about 30; and for every year after that it is 4 years older.

You should see the other guy.

Sled dogs running in the Iditarod burn about 10,000 calories a day.
About 117 dogs have died running the Iditarod over the past 30 years.

I'm burning off that steak. Now about that brownie...

Dogs do not have a collarbone. Their shoulders are disconnected so they can run and leap farther.

Beagles are prone to seizures and epilepsy.

Dogs like to snack out of litter boxes because they are attracted to the protein found in cat poop.

The Giant Irish Wolfhound is so strong that it can pick up a Mastiff with its teeth and shake it to death.

Because they have webbed feet, Newfoundlands are strong swimmers.

Basset Hounds sink straight to the bottom because their legs are too short to tread water.

I did a guy in San Jose. What are you in for?

Dogs take about 10 to 30 breaths per minute.

A dog's heart beats between 70 and 120 times a minute; the human heart beats only 70 to 80 times.

Blowing in a dog's ear can actually damage its hearing. It's not the breeze that hurts but the frequency of the noise. To the dog, the sound is one hundred times worse than running your fingernails down a chalkboard.

I keep saying I'm going to slow down...

Dogs sweat through the pads of their feet.

While most domestic dogs can reach speeds of 20 mph, greyhounds can sprint up to 45 mph.

If its tail is not docked when it is young, a Doberman can wag it so hard that it actually breaks the tailbone.

Great Danes can eat up to 8.5 pounds
of food per day.

Eating daffodils, amaryllis plants, or tulips
can put a dog to go into a coma.

Fifty-two percent of pet owners believe
their pet gets more exercise than
they do.

Don't hate me because I'm beautiful.

It is true that chocolate can be dangerous for dogs. The caffeine can over stimulate their cardiac and nervous systems, but they still love it.

Teddy probably shouldn't have eaten that last piece of chocolate.

Smaller dogs usually have a longer lifespan than larger dogs.

Dogs and humans are the only animals with prostates.

Wild dogs often eat plants, and they also benefit from the vegetable contents in the stomachs of their prey.

There are 18 muscles that help dogs rotate and lift their ears to pinpoint exactly where certain sounds are coming from. They can hear sounds up to 4 times farther away than humans can.

Some veterinarians believe that dogs should never be fed grapes or raisins because doing so will decrease their immunity to plant-borne viruses.

Dogs are often attracted to the sweet taste of antifreeze. Of course, it is highly poisonous.

Similar to Greyhounds, Whippets are often hit by cars because they do not sense the danger of traffic.

Tylenol can be deadly to a dog.

Yum, is that Perrier coming out of my nose?

The Wiener Nationals is a popular Dachshund race occasionally held at greyhound tracks in the U.S.

Because of their short windpipe, French Bulldogs often have trouble breathing.

Some Great Danes develop yeast infections.

Beagles are known to get
separation anxiety.

New research has revealed that dogs are
not colorblind—they simply do not see
detail to the extent that humans do
because the lenses of their eyes are
flatter than humans'.

This migraine just will <u>not</u> go away.

Dogs have three eyelids—an upper lid, a lower lid, and a middle lid that protects the eye from dirt and dust.

Back on the left, see that? It broke while I was eating peanut brittle.

The average dog is born with 28 temporary teeth and eventually develops 42 permanent teeth.

A traditional leash can crush an Affenpinscher's trachea.

A healthy dog can go three to four days without eating.

Cropping a Doberman's ears reduces the chance it will get ear infections or blisters from shaking its head back and forth.

Dachshunds should be discouraged from going up and down stairs and jumping on furniture because of their long spine, short legs, and big bellies. They can break their backs easily.

Basset Hounds were intentionally bred to have dwarfism.

Male dogs mark their territory with urine. The scent tells other dogs in the area both his size and health.

Fire hydrants are so '90s.

Pekinese have very delicate eyes because their eyeballs sit above the eye socket rather than within it.

Get out the SPF 50! Hairless Chinese Crested Dogs are susceptible to both sunburns and acne.

Kelpies have so much energy that they can drive a heard of sheep more than thirty-seven miles uphill.

I can get all the XM channels
with this thing.

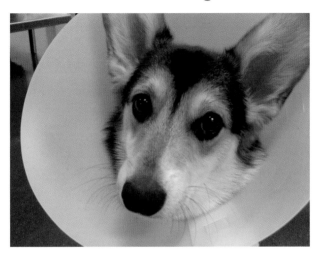

Thirty to forty percent of all solid white
boxers are deaf in at least one ear.

Bloodhounds never have to be bathed.

It's all done with Pilates.

The American Bloodhound Association
is raising money for veterinary schools
to research why the breed is so prone
to bloating.

Most of a Bloodhound's weight is concentrated in its bones, not its fat or muscles.

Because Bernese Mountain dogs do not live very long, the Swiss often say of them, "Three years a young dog, three years a good dog, three years an old dog."

Thirty to forty percent of all the pets in the United States are overweight.

Puppies are usually born 63 days after conception.

You've got a little piece of chocolate right...there. No—or is that...?

Labrador Retrievers are known to eat anything that isn't nailed to the floor.

Chihuahuas, however, are picky eaters.

If born with an unusually large head, Chihuahuas can die from hydrocephalus, or water on the brain. They are also known for having soft spots in their skulls.

Dogs with floppy ears often get ear infections because moist air gets trapped in the ear canal.

Some veterinarians use natural remedies, prescribing:
Aloe: to help with itching.
Echinacea: to strengthen the immune system.
Ginger: to relieve tummy problems.
St. John's Wart: to fight off viruses.

EXTRA, EXTRA, BREED ALL ABOUT IT!

Chow Chows were originally bred not only for entertainment but also for food.

The French Bulldog often requires a Caesarean section to give birth.

In nineteenth-century France, prostitutes often carried French Bulldogs around as a secret code to let potential customers know their profession.

I can't believe that bitch is wearing the same outfit.

Two dogs survived the sinking of the *Titanic*—Henry Sleeper Harper's Pekingese and Margaret Hays' Pomeranian.

Dachshunds were originally bred to go into badger dens and fight the badgers.

If a talented racing-lead dog, the Alaskan Husky can sell for $10,000-15,000.

The Lundehund, a breed restricted solely to Norway, has 5 toes and 7 or 8 cushions on the bottom of each foot.

Bulldogs were bred to fight bulls
and bears.

The first Shar-Pei to ever arrive in the
U.S. was named Kung Fu.

Mixed-breed dogs were banned from
obedience contests until the 1980s.

There are only about 8,000 Eurasiers in
the entire world.

The Jack Russell Terrier was first bred by Reverend John Russell, who bought a small brown and white terrier named Trump from his milkman while in college.

Leave my ears out of this.

Clumber Spaniels are known for their sneaky ways of raiding the kitchen cabinet and for always needing to carry something around in their mouths—like a shoe.

Here's your remote, now get me a beer.

Border Collies are often used to chase wild birds off golf courses and airport runways.

The Boxer was named after the way it plays with and provokes other dogs with its front paws.

In the U.S., the most common dog put up for adoption is the American Pit Bull Terrier.

There are 701 types of purebred dogs.

Great Pyrenees are so sensitive to anesthesia that it can kill them.

The Afghan Hound's name can be translated as "baboon" or "monkey-faced hound."

The Basenji does not bark.

Bloodhounds do not get their name from an ability to smell blood. It means "blooded hound," or aristocratic.

If you kids don't settle down, I'm going to have to pull over!

Some prize-winning purebred dogs have genetic defects due to inbreeding.

In New York City, the Poodle was the most registered breed of dog in 2005.

Anyone got the trifecta results?

When dog names are combined after crossbreeding, the results are often quite funny…

Puggle—Beagle/Pug

Labradoodle—Labrador Retriever/Standard Poodle

Bogle—Boxer/Beagle

Cockapoo—Cocker Spaniel/Poodle

Shollie—German Shepherd/Rough Collie

Some Border Collie breeders are superstitious that their dogs should not be mostly red or white.

St. Bernards were first called Saint Dogs and Barry Dogs.

Early drawings of St. Bernards often include a barrel of liquor tied around their necks. Because they were traditionally rescue dogs, the brandy was supposed to help warm the people found in the snow. However, the monks who trained the animal deny this was ever true.

Today the Africanis breed is still found amidst traditional South African tribes.

A girl needs her beauty sleep.

The Chinese once used Shar-Peis for
fighting dogs, but they are so laid back
the men had to drug them to make
them violent.

Beagles' tails are most useful when wagging in the air to help hunters find the short canines in the field.

Beagles can be trained to sniff out termites.

Basset hounds can pick up a better scent on a damp morning.

Puppies bred by well-certified breeders rarely end up in shelters.

OUTRAGEOUS
PET OWNERS

When Lord Byron's dog, Boatswain, died, the poet was so devastated that he wrote a touching epitaph for the canine's headstone: "Beauty without vanity, strength without insolence, courage without ferocity, and all the virtues of man without his vices."

Royalty used to keep their dogs under the covers in hopes that fleas and bedbugs would stay away from their legs and bite their furry friends instead.

What's the number for 911 again?

A new cell phone in the shape of a bone can be connected to a dog's collar so owners can talk to the pet while away from home.

At $1.5 billion, people spend 4 times more money on pet food than they do on baby food every year.

Jerome Napoleon Bonaparte died of injuries from tripping over his dog's leash in 1945.

More than 40 percent of pet owners admit they talk to their canine friends over the telephone.

One quarter of all pet owners blow-dry their pet's hair after giving it a bath.

Some people believe that if they hear a dog barking first thing in the morning, it is a sign of misfortune.

Before New York City made it mandatory for owners to clean up after their pets, 40 million pounds of dog excrement were deposited on the streets there every year.

The famed Paris pet cemetery Cimetiere des Chiens opened in 1899 and although it translates as "Cemetery of Dogs," there are horses, lions, fish, and even monkeys buried there. The expensive plots belong to famed actor Rin Tin Tin and pets of several celebrities. In 1987, the French government declared the cemetery a historical monument.

How did you know I was here?

Half of all dog owners give their pet a human name.

Kublai Khan of the Yuan dynasty owned five thousand mastiffs at one time!

Yes, I'm playing Vegas all week.

Ancient Chinese royalty used to carry their dogs around in the oversized sleeves of their robes.

Poshintang, or Dog Meat Soup, is a popular dish on Korean menus. It is believed to improve a woman's complexion and cure health problems related to the heat of the summer.

Forty percent of dog and cat owners admit to carrying a picture of their pet in their wallet.

In the U.S., 1 million dogs are named as the primary beneficiary in their owner's wills.

Originally, owners of Dachshunds used the dog's long tail to help pull it out of burrow holes after it chased down a badger.

Senior citizens who own dogs visit the doctor 21 percent fewer times than seniors without dogs.

Nursing homes for the elderly that allow pets such as dogs, cats, and birds experience 21 percent fewer deaths than other nursing homes.

And now we shall begin the traditional folk ritual of the ancient mountain weirdos.

Some owners tattoo ID codes on their dogs' bellies.

Others implant microchips with GPS tracking capabilities.

A 2001 study revealed that 80 percent of pet owners feed their animal friends food from the dinner table.

Pet owners tend to have lower cholesterol than non-pet owners.

Pekinese were bred intentionally bowlegged in China because the Emperor and eunuchs wanted to discourage them from wandering away.

What, no more cake?

Some owners take their Dachshunds to an acupuncturist and chiropractor or give them arthritis medicine like Rimadyl to relieve back pain.

Mirror, mirror, on the car, who has the biggest nose of them all?

WACKY LAWS
ABOUT DOGS

In Paulding, Ohio, it is legal for a policeman to bite a dog to make it stop barking.

Dogs in Pennsylvania seeking to congregate in groups of three or more on private property must first have a permit signed by the mayor.

A California City Council passed an ordinance that read, "No dog shall be in a public place without its master on a leash."

It is illegal to "educate" dogs in Hartford, Connecticut.

Stay outta this alley or I'll break your milkbone.

Making faces at dogs is against the law in Normal, Illinois.

Airlines will not ship Shih Tzus because they are so sensitive to high temperatures that they will likely not survive the flight.

Dogs are prohibited from flying kites on most public beaches in the United States.

In Ventura County, California, it's illegal for cats and dogs to have intercourse without a permit.

In ancient Egypt, a man who killed a Greyhound received the same punishment as a man who killed another person.

In Iceland, it was once against the law to have a pet dog.

Because Kaiser Wilhelm II was such a fan of the breed, Dachshunds were stoned to death in England during World War I. Americans even used them in political cartoons to poke fun at Germany.

Is this how you do the Shag?

Giving a lit cigar to a dog will get you
thrown in jail in Zion, Illinois.

Those tulip bulbs are tickling my butt.

Law enforcement dogs are protected by laws that prohibit pedestrians from distracting them from doing their job.

The dogs also cannot be prosecuted for biting on the job.

Some cities require pet owners to scoop their own yard within 24 hours after their dog has relieved itself there.

It is illegal for dogs and cats to fight in Barber, North Carolina.

It is against the law to keep wild Dingoes as pets in some parts of the world, but many owners simply register them as Kelpies, which are a cross between Dingoes and Collies.

Before it was made illegal, Boxers were often used for street dogfights.

Some cities fine pet owners $25 to $1000 for not abiding by poop scoop laws.

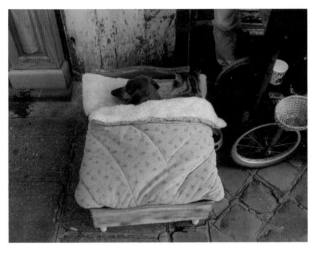

Sleeping with the enemy.

Dog theft is considered theft of personal property.

It is illegal to crop a dog's ears in the United Kingdom.

Owners cannot take their French Poodles to the opera in Chicago.

Et tu, Brute?

It is illegal to give a dog whiskey
in Illinois.

In Ohio there are no laws requiring
kennels to exercise dogs.

In California, antifreeze manufacturers
have to increase the amount of ethylene
glycol in their product to make it bitter
and deter dogs from licking it up off
garage floors. Wholesale products,
however, are exempt from the law—
which is mostly what car mechanics use.

In California, dogs are banned from mating within 1,500 feet of a school or a place of worship.

Airlines are required to feed and give water to dogs in flight every 24 hours. Puppies must be checked on every 12 hours.

Puppies under 8 weeks old cannot be taken on an airplane.

Uh, Cledus, I think I'm stuck.

One million people spend 10 minutes
reading www.dogbitelaw.com every year.

Dogs may not bark for more than fifteen
minutes in Northbrook, Illinois.

The Puppy Lemon Law allows new owners in some states to return their dog if they find out it is sick.

Dogs may not molest cars in Fort Thomas, Kentucky.

I wish someone'd told me sooner this thing had a back door.

Laws protect circuses, zoos, and research laboratories from vandalism and trespassing of animal rights groups like PETA.

In Connecticut a law was almost passed to restrict how much time dogs are forced to spend outside, but it was dropped under the presumption that it was "excessive intrusion" into voters' lives.

The "one bite rule" shields dog owners from liability the first time their pet bites someone.

People who make "ugly faces" at dogs
may be fined in Oklahoma.

It is illegal to kill a dog using a
decompression chamber in Michigan.

Owners cannot tie their pet to the roof
of a car.

MODEL BEHAVIOR: SECRETS OF CANINE PRIMPING

The pom-pom puffs of fur left on the feet and tail of Poodles were originally intended to keep the dogs' joints warm when they went swimming.

I feel so pretty and witty and gay!

Too much white on an Australian Shepherd's fur often means it is deaf or blind.

Ladies and Gentlemen, the Sultan of Brunei.

A saddle, or blanket, coat of fur means that there is a second color only over the center of the back.

To get tar, paint, or oil off a dog without having to cut its fur, simply rub peanut butter onto the stained spot, let it dry, then brush out with a comb.

Poodle fur grows so constantly that it requires more frequent trimming than that of other breeds.

Dalmatians are not born with spots—
they appear with age.

Dog show handlers frequently shave off
the canine's chin whiskers.

Next time I'll remember
the sunscreen.

Handlers also are known to wrap up the ends of dogs' fur to keep it from getting tangled before their shining moment on stage.

American Cocker Spaniels are categorized into three colors—black, mixed colors, and ASCOB, which stands for Any Solid Color Other than Black.

According to the Institute for the Study of Animal Problems, dogs, like people, are either right-handed or left-handed. They favor one paw over the other.

In London, the Dog's Toilet Club pampers pets with egg yolk shampoos, evening gowns, and even a chiropractor.

Some breeds have two coats of fur—a soft undercoat and a rough topcoat. Most shed their undercoat each spring, commonly called "blowing the coat."

Legend holds that the Chow Chow got its blue tongue by licking up a drop of paint the day that God painted the sky blue.

Shar-Peis also have black and
blue tongues.

Judges at dog shows consider the
canine's color, markings, pattern, texture,
and length of fur.

No, I don't know who peed in the
swimming pool.

Australian Shepherds often have two different colored eyes or bi-colored eyes, where each eye is half-brown and half-blue.

In 2003, GroomTeam USA won the silver medal at the World Groom Team Championships.

When racing in the snow, Alaskan Huskies often wear dog booties to keep their feet from getting hurt.

Some day my prince will come.

If it has ears that do not stand straight up or a muzzle that is not completely black, the German Shepherd will be disqualified in a show competition.

The Labradoodle (Labrador Retriever/Poodle) and the Goldendoodle (Golden Retriever/Poodle) were originally bred because they shed very little and can be owned by people with allergies.

Here's looking at you, kid.

If you clip the fur of a Border Terrier, especially around its back, the fur will turn curly and never look the same again.

London groomer R.W. Brown has cut battle scenes and family crests into Poodle fur.

Because it comes from a long line of dogs that work around water, Chesapeake Bay Retrievers have an oily coat that is almost waterproof.

Several breeds of dogs have webbed feet—Newfoundland, Labrador Retriever, Poodle, Field Spaniel, and more!

Breeders believe that Rottweilers should have spots on their cheeks and eyebrows, and each toe should have a little black line that looks like a pencil marking.

The name Shar-Pei translates into "Sand Skin"—not because of its sandy brown color but because of the rough texture of the dog's skin.

Because of their underbite, Boxers often get their teeth caught in their jowls.

Most baby Pugs have a black "mask" around their face.

You mean that fat man is just the chimney sweep?

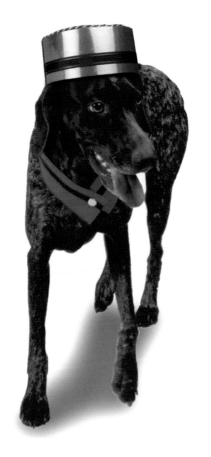

May I take your bags, ma'am?

DOGS IN

HISTORY

The earliest fossils found of dogs date back to at least 10,000 BC.

The Bloodhound was frequently used to track down runaway slaves.

After its owner died and his casket was shipped East on the Great Northern Railroad, a Collie named Shep met every train at the station, sniffing for his old friend. He did this for six years until he was run over by one of the trains.

Fort Benson, Montana honored Shep on the fiftieth anniversary of his death by raising $100,000 for a statue. Sculptor Bob Scriver crafted the dog in bronze.

King Henry III of France carried his Bichon puppy in a basket everywhere he went.

Lhasa Apso originated in Lhasa, the capital of Tibet. During World War I, however, the breed shrank down to only thirty in the entire country.

Lhasa Apso were once used by monks
to guard temples. They were considered
spiritually valuable and good luck in
800 BC.

Once upon a time, there was a dashing
Dalmatian...

Tax collector Louis Doberman bred the first Doberman to protect him on the job.

I love being Ralph Lauren's dog.

The Irish Wolfhound was once a pet owned strictly by nobility, emperors, and kings.

Legend holds that the Pekinese was formed when a lion fell in love with a marmoset and asked Buddha to shrink him down to be the same size as his mate.

Another legend states that the Pekinese actually comes from mating a lion and a monkey.

Napoleon Bonaparte's wife, Josephine, loved her Pug, Fortune, so much that she insisted it sleep in their bed—even on their wedding night. "If the Pug doesn't sleep in our bed, neither do I!" she insisted.

In the mid-1930s, the Nazi party believed White German Shepherd dogs to be inferior, believing that the white coat was a sign of degeneration. To this day, they remain ineligible for registration as German Shepherds within Germany and throughout Europe. They refer to them simply as White Shepherds.

Off with their heads!

After being accused of accepting illegal gifts in politics, President Nixon went on television with his dog, Checkers, admitting that the canine was the only thing he ever accepted from lobbyists. He then refused to return the dog, even if it was considered a crime.

At one time, all the Havanese dogs in the United States could be traced back to the original thirteen dogs brought into the country by Bert and Dorothy Goodale.

The Norrbottenspets were declared extinct by the Swedish Kennel Club in 1948, but were reinstated in 1967 when it was discovered the breed was actually alive and thriving.

Has anyone seen my glasses?

Do not be afraid. We have come to your planet to help you.

Believed to be the reincarnation of lions, Bernese Mountain Dogs were originally used in Switzerland to herd cows and haul carts full of milk jars and farm equipment.

During World War I, Boxers were used in the military as messengers, guard dogs, and pack-carriers.

Adolf Hitler wanted to breed a guard dog, but when he was introduced to the Bouvier des Flandres, it bit him on the hand. He ordered that every canine of that breed be exterminated.

Chihuahuas were brought to Mexico by Spanish settlers.

Aztec Indians believed the Mexican Hairless Dog, or Xolos, would help their souls safely through the underworld.

Today some still believe the breed has healing powers and telepathic abilities. Cultures other than the Aztecs ate the Mexican Hairless Dog for medicinal purposes.

Ancient Egyptians worshiped a dog god named Anubis, the "Lord of the Afterlife."

Always a bridesmaid, never a bride.

King Tutankhamen was buried with his dog, Abuwitiyuh, for company and protection in the afterlife.

Sorry kid, you have to get past us for the candy.

Soviet leader Nikita Khrushchev gave
First Lady Jacqueline Kennedy a pet dog
named Pushinka.

Franklin D. Roosevelt once spent
$15,000 ordering a ship to return to the
Aleutian Islands to get his Scottie dog,
which had been left behind.

George Washington had thirty-six
foxhounds, one by the name
of "Sweetlips."

When the city of Ashkelon was excavated, a cemetery with 700 dog graves was found. Researchers assumed the culture had worshiped the animals as healers because when dogs licked a wound, it healed faster.

A rare group in the Philippines believes that the world was created by the god of the sky, Kabigat. Kabigat came to earth with his dogs to hunt, but had to create hills and mountains to locate them by the echoes of their barks.

Lyndon B. Johnson's public image was hurt when photos of him yanking his dog up by the ears circulated in the media.

I can't believe I fell for
this one—again.

King Eystein, ruler of Norway between 1104 and 1123, was exiled and asked his countrymen to choose their new king—either his slave or his dog. They chose his dog, Suening.

Beware the evil eye.

When "town mooch" Shorty of Fairplay, Colorado died in 1951, his dog, Bum, was so depressed that he lay on his master's grave and refused to eat or drink until he died as well.

Some of the earliest drawings in existence portray men with dogs. The oldest known drawing of this kind was found in Persia (now Iran) and dates back to 7000 BC.

In Africa, the Nandi tribe believes that death originated from a dog. A canine allegedly once asked someone in the village for a sip of milk through a straw, but it was instead offered to him in a bowl. Upset, he created death.

Islam's Mohammed is said to have owned a dog, although traditionally his religion taught that the animal was so impure that even touching one required "purification." He believed that only Allah could destroy all dogs, although he did like the idea of doing off with black dogs with light marks above the eyes—which was considered a sign of the devil.

In Judaism, dogs are considered unclean. When the Torah was written, dogs often traveled in packs, nosed through public garbage cans, and carried diseases.

For many years, I, Miss Higginbotham, have been teaching little children that they are very, very bad.

The first animal shelters in the U.S. were built in the 1700s, but they were only used to house stray animals waiting to be euthanized.

Teddy Roosevelt's Pit Bull, Pete, bit and ripped the pants of a French ambassador at a White House event.

Odysseus' dog, Argus, was said to have recognized his master after 19 years of absence.

STRANGE BUT TRUE: RANDOM FACTS

Smiling at a dog may make it attack you. To many breeds, showing your teeth is a sign of aggression.

A Miniature Dachshund named Brutus is the only animal approved by the Humane Society and his own veterinarian for skydiving.

Fur from Border Collies, Chows, Shih Tzus, and Samoyeds can be used for knitting.

Nose prints can identify dogs in the same way fingerprints identify humans. They are often kept on file with insurance companies.

Dogs most likely dream while they are asleep.

Dogs are least popular in Switzerland and Germany, where only one in ten families have the pet.

OK, I'll chew it, but I'd rather have a steak dinner.

Dogs drool when they are nervous, excited, or are anticipating their next meal. Giving them a chew toy can help them swallow and stop the mess.

The five most popular male dog names are Max, Jake, Buddy, Bailey, and Sam. The five most popular female names are Maggie, Molly, Lady, Sadie, and Lucy.

Just call me Tink.

It costs approximately $6,400 to raise a medium-sized dog to the age of 11.

In Hawaii, mixed breed dogs—or mutts—are referred to as "poi dog."

In Brazil, mutts are referred to as "vira-lata," which loosely translates into "taking out the garbage" because the pups are known to knock over trash cans searching for food on the streets.

Dogs have about 7,000 fewer taste buds than humans do, but they make up for the loss with their excellent sense of smell.

Dogs have nearly 220 million smell-sensitive cells—44 times more than humans.

Chihuahuas are so jealous that they will resent their owners for close human relationships.

The all-time best-selling children's dog books are:
1) *The Poky Little Puppy* (1942)
2) *Where the Red Fern Grows* (1973)
3) *The Incredible Journey* (1984)
4) *Fox in Socks* (1965)
Clifford the Big Red Dog came in 10th.

Jeesh, I should be making at least minimum wage for this.

Minnesota has the largest population of Gray Wolves in the U.S.

Wait—there she is! Miss Furry
Des Moines!

There are 2,917 puppies and kittens
born every hour. That is 7 times the
human birth rate.

About 914 people go to the emergency room with dog bites every day in the U.S.

When one breeds a Bandog with another Bandog, the puppies are not Bandog.

The number one reason pets are given up to shelters is because the owners are moving.

Because they are so hyper, Pugs are called "Multo in Parvo," which means "a lot of dog in a small space."

One female dog and her offspring can produce 67,000 dogs in only 6 years.

If separated from their owners for long periods of time, Bloodhounds will pout and stop eating.

When Labrador Retrievers swim, their fur is waterproof and their tails act as a rudder, directing them through the water.

I never did get the point of this stupid game.

If they swim too frequently, Labs can develop "swimtail," a condition where their tail gets swollen.

Maybe one day I'll be out of the baby pool.

Puppies often lick their mother's mouth to beg for food.

Dog Canyon in Texas' Big Bend National Park was named by an early traveler who saw a dog guarding a wagon in the canyon.

New Guinea Singing Dogs howl like wolves but change the pitch of the howl frequently, giving them their name.

In Finland, hunting dogs have cell phones strapped to them so owners can issue verbal commands from far away.

Some female dogs lift both hind legs to urinate on objects behind them.

Most dogs consider anything given by hand to be a treat—even a piece of dry dog food served at every meal.

As many as 6 to 8 million dogs and cats are put in shelters every year in the U.S., but there are only about 6,000 shelters.